Clywd's Lost Railw

Neil Burgess

Brymbo West Crossing Halt, *c.* 1905.

Text © Neil Burgess, 2022
First published in the United Kingdom, 2022,
by Stenlake Publishing Ltd.
www.stenlake.co.uk
ISBN 978-1-84033-927-7

Printed by
Blissetts, Unit E1-E8 Shield Drive,
West Cross Ind Pk, Brentford, TW8 9EX

Picture Credits

The publishers would like to thank John Alsop for the cover photographs, and those
on pages 1, 2, 6, 7, 12, 18-24, 29-38, 41-43, 47-49, 51 and 53.

The signal box at Llandderfel on the Rhiwabon/Ruabon – Dolgellau line, *c.* 1906.

Introduction

The county of Clwyd was a product of the 1974 reorganisation of local government in England and Wales, which in Wales attempted to create new county authorities with populations of around half a million people. It comprised the old counties of Denbigh and Flint, which were themselves a creation of an older reorganisation of government in Wales, being imposed after the English attempt to subdue the country after 1282. Clwyd was to have only a brief existence as a local authority, being abolished as a functioning unit in 1996 when it was replaced by the 'single-tier' authorities of Flintshire, Denbighshire and Wrecsam County Borough, a small part in the west going to Conwy. However, it still exists as a 'preserved county', still having a Lord Lieutenant and existing for certain ceremonial functions. In 2003 the boundary of the preserved county was revised to include all of Conwy County Borough.

Clywd was the only 1974 county not to take the name of one of the old Welsh princedoms, having originally been the northern part of Powys. In the time of the princes, on its western border was Gwynedd, the historic stronghold of Welsh identity and nationhood and the most resistant to Norman expansion. After 1270 the English under Edward I built a network of castles, often called the 'Ring of Iron', across northern and mid-Wales in an attempt both to subjugate the population and to create islands of English language and culture in towns which grew up in their shadows. Thus in what was to become Clwyd, Flint, Hawarden, Rhyddlan and Denbigh arose; but Wales before the Industrial Revolution was not an urban society beyond the very limited reach of these and other English settlements and Clwyd inherited this rural character through much of its area.

The most notable exception to this was the town of Wrecsam – anglicised to Wrexham – which after 1282 became the administrative centre of the Marcher Lordship of Bromfield and Yale and a town of considerable importance. Just how important it was is indicated by St Giles' church, its nave built in the fourteenth century and its 180-foot tower started in 1506, which dominates the centre of the town and appears in many photographs of Wrexham Central station. Industry came early to Wrecsam, with ironworks being established at Bersham in the seventeenth century which cast cannon for use in the Civil Wars. Coal,

iron and later steel, bricks and limestone were staples of the area as the Industrial Revolution gathered pace after 1750 and the river navigation along the Dyfrwydwy/Dee and Mersey allowed trade inwards and outwards. As with many other parts of Britain, the mid-twentieth century saw the decline and eventual extinction of all or most of these industries, with the virtual disappearance of almost any trace of them in many places by the early years of the twenty-first century.

Railways grew up naturally alongside industrialisation. Navigable rivers and the Shropshire Union Canal gave rise to a number of horse-worked tramroads built as feeders and the Buckley Railway was a much longer and more significant line north of Wrecsam which lasted well into the twentieth century; but none of these were passenger lines, so are beyond the scope of this book. The development of passenger railways worked by steam power saw the arrival in north-east Wales of the two great English companies, the Great Western and the London & North

Wrexham Exchange Station built by the Wrexham, Mold & Connah's Quay Railway. The station was merged with the adjacent Wrexham General in 1981. The buildings have now been demolished.

Western, both of which absorbed more local undertakings, the Shrewsbury & Chester and the Chester & Holyhead, respectively. They created a network of lines which supported passenger traffic into the twentieth century but mainly were reliant on goods services, which survived until the middle of the twentieth century with some lasting right up until the disappearance of extractive and heavy industries in the area.

Even more lines were projected during the nineteenth century but never built. They had designs on the coalfield area, though others also contended for a share of the spoils. Paradoxically it is one of these, the Wrexham, Mold & Connah's Quay, which provides the most complete route still existing in the area to the west of the Shrewsbury & Chester main line, linking Wrecsam to the Wirral and Liverpool. Because its passenger lines remain largely intact it features very little in this account, though it linked with a number of the closed lines described later. It was the WM&CQR which saw the intervention in north-east Wales of the Manchester, Sheffield & Lincolnshire Railway, later the Great Central (and, after 1923, a constituent of the London & North Eastern).

Away from the industrial area, railways stretched out into the countryside, along the prosperous agricultural Vale of Clwyd and across the thinly-populated land of mid-Wales, through Llangollen and onwards to Bala and the coast beyond Dolgellau. From Bala too there ran one of the most spectacular secondary lines of the old Great Western system, winding its way through the mountains to a bleak summit at Cwn Prysor, through Trawsfynedd – literally 'across the mountain' – and down into the capital of the slate industry in Blaenau Ffestiniog. Meanwhile along the coast ran the London & North Western route to Caergybi/Holyhead, chosen early on in the nineteenth century as the packet port for Dublin and a vital link in the Westminster government's attempts to rule Ireland before its eventual independence – apart from the six northern counties – in 1921. Of the two, the LNWR route has survived and serves a coastal strip from which much of the industry has departed but which is increasingly popular as a holiday resort and place of settlement in later life for many people from Manchester, Liverpool and north-west England. The Great Western line, though long closed as a through route, survives in part as not one but two preserved railways; the standard gauge Llangollen Railway from Llangollen to Corwen and the Rheilffordd Llyn Tegid/Bala Lake Railway between Bala and Llanwchllyn. Much has gone, but there is still much to see and, better still, to travel over.

The Welsh Language

Throughout the nineteenth and well into the twentieth centuries the railway companies of Britain were notoriously anglophone in outlook and in Wales generally paid scant regard to the language. This included not only the lines of the predominantly English companies like the London & North Western, Great Western and Midland, but also the indigenous Welsh undertakings, including even the Cambrian, whose lines traversed the predominantly Welsh-speaking areas of mid and north Wales. The most obvious manifestation of this disregard of Welsh – an outlook reflecting that of government – was the anglicising of place names, either by revising the spelling or substituting English names for the Welsh originals. Illustrations of the first kind covered by this book are Wrexham for Wrecsam (there is no X in the Welsh alphabet) or Ruabon for Rhiwabon; the second kind is shown by abbreviating Rhosllanerchrugog to Rhos or changing Trefynnon to Holywell.

From the 1960s onwards, a revaluing of the Welsh language required public bodies to embrace bilingualism, including the use of signs in both Welsh and English. This included railways and Welsh stations have seen the use of historic names alongside the English versions by which they were formerly known. To recognise this, the titles in this book use both while the text and the names of stations and companies use the names and spellings by which they were known in the period, since many stations and lines closed before this policy could be implemented.

Closure Dates

This book lists dates when stations and lines were closed to regular scheduled passenger traffic. Readers need to recognise that sources vary in deciding closure dates, some giving the last day on which regular services operated, others the first day when closure was effected and no passenger traffic operated. Especially on lines with no regular Sunday service, this might yield a discrepancy of two days, depending on the method used. In some cases, particularly before the mid 1960s, stations along closed lines were left substantially intact and periodically excursion trains called to pick up or set down passengers. In the case of at least one line in this book, a closed route was used for regular excursion traffic in the form of the 'North Wales Land Cruise'. Where sources indicate that these arrangements existed they may be noted in the text, however the official closure date will still be given.

Railways of Clwyd

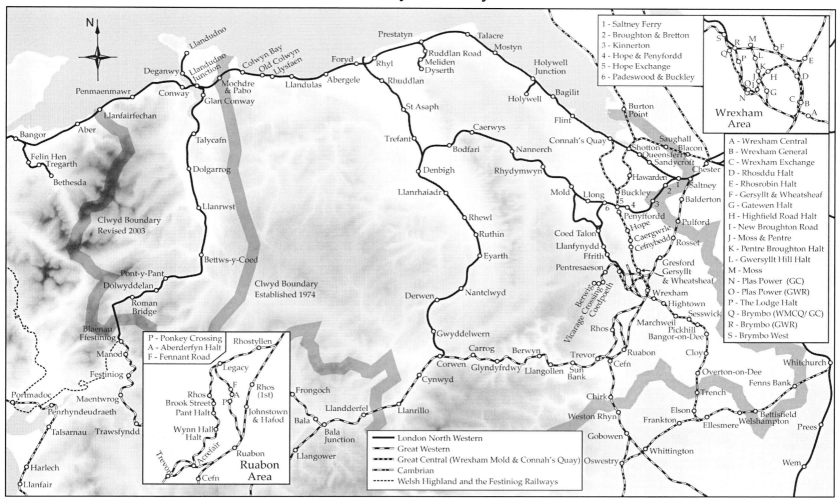

N

1 - Saltney Ferry
2 - Broughton & Bretton
3 - Kinnerton
4 - Hope & Penyfordd
5 - Hope Exchange
6 - Padeswood & Buckley

Wrexham Area

A - Wrexham Central
B - Wrexham General
C - Wrexham Exchange
D - Rhosddu Halt
E - Rhosrobin Halt
F - Gersyllt & Wheatsheaf
G - Gatewen Halt
H - Highfield Road Halt
I - New Broughton Road
J - Moss & Pentre
K - Pentre Broughton Halt
L - Gwersyllt Hill Halt
M - Moss
N - Plas Power (GC)
O - Plas Power (GWR)
P - The Lodge Halt
Q - Brymbo (WMCQ/ GC)
R - Brymbo (GWR)
S - Brymbo West

P - Ponkey Crossing
A - Aberderfyn Halt
F - Fennant Road

Ruabon Area

London North Western
Great Western
Great Central (Wrexham Mold & Connah's Quay)
Cambrian
Welsh Highland and the Festiniog Railways

Relief shading contains OS data © Crown copyright and database right 2022.

Chester – Yr Wyddgrug/Mold – Dynbych/Denbigh

Passenger service withdrawn	30 April 1962
Distance	29¼ miles
Original owning company	The Mold Railway / Mold & Denbigh Junction Railway

Station closed	Date of closure
Saltney Ferry	30 April 1962
Broughton & Bretton *	30 April 1962
Kinnerton	30 April 1962
Hope & Penyffordd **	30 April 1962
Hope Low Level ***	1 September 1958
Padeswood & Buckley ****	6 January 1958
Llong†	30 April 1962
Mold	30 April 1962

Station closed	Date of closure
Rhydymwyn	30 April 1962
Star Crossing Halt	30 April 1962
Nannerch	30 April 1962
Caerwys	30 April 1962
Bodfari	30 April 1962

* Originally named Broughton until April 1861, then named Broughton Hall until 1 July 1908.
** Originally named Hope until 16 January 1912.
*** Originally named Hope Exchange until 7 November 1953.
**** Originally named Padeswood until 1 February 1874.
† Closed temporarily from 1 January 1917 to 5 May 1919.

Mold Junction looking east towards Chester. On the right are the platforms of Saltney Ferry Station and the sheds of the locomotive depot.

London, Midland and Scottish Railway locomotive No. 6624 at Kinnerton Station.

A number of railway schemes were promoted to connect Mold to the Chester & Holyhead Railway during the 'Railway Mania' of the 1840s. The line that was actually built ran from Saltney Junction to Mold and was named the Mold Railway, incorporated by an Act of July 1847. The line was engineered by Peto & Betts, one of the great contracting firms of the period. The railway opened on 14 August 1849 and was worked from the outset by the London & North Western Railway, which by then had absorbed the Chester & Holyhead Railway. The first seven and a quarter miles were double track and the remaining two and three quarters miles single. Considerable mineral traffic was carried from the outset.

Hope Low Level Station, May 1955.

The opening of the Vale of Clwyd Railway in October 1858 (see page 39), and the interest shown in it from the outset by the LNWR, led to the promotion of the Mold & Denbigh Junction Railway, which was incorporated by an Act of August 1861. The line was constructed by Richard France of Shrewsbury, another engineer with long associations with north-east and mid Wales. Work started in August 1864 but troubles in the financial markets, including the collapse of Overend, Gurney, a banking firm which had financed a number of railway projects, slowed progress and it was August 1869 before the fifteen miles were opened. The LNWR worked it from the outset, though the company retained its nominal independence until the Grouping of 1923. In due course a good deal of the traffic over the Denbigh–Corwen line originated or terminated in Chester and both lines closed to passengers on 30 April 1962.

Mold Station, 1924.

Rhydymwyn Station, May 1961.

Star Crossing Halt, May 1961.

Nannerch Station, *c.* 1905.

Bodfari Station, May 1961.

Ellesmere – Wrecsam/Wrexham *

Passenger service withdrawn	8 September 1962
Distance	12¾ miles
Original owning company	Wrexham & Ellesmere Railway

Stations closed	Date of closure
Elson Halt	8 September 1962
Trench Halt	8 September 1962
Overton-on-Dee	8 September 1962
Cloy Halt **	8 September 1962
Bangor-on-Dee	8 September 1962

Station closed	Date of closure
Pickhill Halt	8 September 1962
Sesswick Halt	8 September 1962
Marchweil	8 September 1962
Hightown Halt ***	8 September 1962

* All stations closed between 10 June 1940 and 6 May 1946.
** Originally named Caedyah Halt until 1932.
*** Also known as Hightown Platform.

Overton-on-Dee Station.

The Oswestry, Ellesmere & Whitchurch Railway was promoted in 1861 (see separate section) to link those towns and to provide a connection between the Oswestry & Newtown Railway to the rest of the national network. In the fullness of time, both these companies became constituents of the Cambrian Railways, along with the Newtown & Machynlleth Railway and the Aberystwyth & Welch [*sic*] Coast Railway. However, there was a good deal of interest in linking the Oswestry, Ellesmere & Whitchurch to either Ruabon or Wrexham, though for decades these proposals failed to come to fruition.

However, there was also interest in creating a line to connect Ellesmere to the Wrexham, Mold & Connah's Quay Railway, which ran north from Wrecsam to the Dee at Connah's Quay. The WM&CQ was a struggling company serving a section of the Flintshire coalfield, but it had considerable ambitions though few came to fruition. One of these was a line from Wrecsam to Welshampton, which was considered from 1882 and obtained a parliamentary Act two years later. However, the idea was not forgotten and when the company came into the orbit of the Manchester, Sheffield & Lincolnshire Railway, a new possibility emerged.

There had long been an ambition to provide a north-south railway link through Wales which would be able to compete with the London & North Western and Great Western companies, not least in the jointly owned line up through the borders linking Newport and Birkenhead. The MS&LR board was chaired by the redoubtable Sir Edward Watkin, a man of wide-ranging ambition who, among other projects, sought to construct a channel tunnel linking Britain to France. In Wales there was the nucleus of a north–south link by the 1890s, including the Brecon & Merthyr and the Cambrian companies, but a 'missing link' was a section to join the Oswestry–Whitchurch line to Wrecsam. Watkin applied his influence to the scheme and in August 1888 an

Marchweil Station.

Act was passed for the building of the Wrexham & Ellesmere Railway, notionally independent but intended to be worked by the Cambrian and to provide a penultimate connection in the north.

The line opened on 2 November 1895, construction having taken longer than anticipated and requiring a parliamentary extension of time permitted for the works. The route made an end-on connection with the WM&CQ line at Wrecsam and did indeed carry traffic for the north-south Wales link, though this never amounted to a great deal in view of the long and tortuous journey through the hills of mid Wales. The Cambrian worked the line from the outset, ordering three neat 0-4-4 tank engines from Naysmyth, Wilson of Manchester for the task, which became the '3' class. In the years before the Great War the Cambrian experimented with push-pull operation and this set a pattern for the way the passenger service was to be operated for much of the line's existence. The line gave the Cambrian access to the largest town on its system and carried some of the products of the north Wales coalfield, an environment not normally associated with the company.

The Wrexham & Ellesmere remained an independent company until the Grouping when it was absorbed, along with the Cambrian, into the reconstituted Great Western Railway. The GWR instituted a number of economies during the 1920s, removing the station staff from Overton on Dee and Bangor on Dee, leaving only the signalmen. However new halts were opened at Cloy in June 1932, Elson in February 1937 and Pickhill in May 1938. After the fall of France in 1940 a new ordnance factory was built at Marchweil which was rail connected. To avoid unnecessary complications in transporting workers and supplies the public passenger service was withdrawn 'for the duration' from 8 June 1940 and was not reinstated until May 1946, local passengers being conveyed by a bus service.

The line was badly hit by road competition and although it generated considerable goods traffic during the war and beyond, Marchweil ordnance factory's production gradually diminished during the 1950s. Passenger services eventually ceased from 8 September 1962 and the line was closed completely and lifted south of Pickhill two months later. The northern end remained as a goods line, though with gradually diminishing traffic. The remainder of the line closed completely from May 1981, fourteen years short of its centenary.

Holywell Junction – Holywell Town

Passenger service withdrawn	6 September 1954
Distance	1½ miles
Original owning company	Holywell Railway

Station closed	*Date of closure*
St Winefride's Halt	6 September 1954
Holywell Town	6 September 1954

Holywell Junction Station on the main Chester to Bangor line was opened as Holywell in 1848. When the branch line to Holywell was opened in 1912 it became Holywell Junction. It closed to passengers on 14 February 1966. It is one of the sites being considered for a new station to serve the surrounding communities.

St Winefride's Halt.

L. & N. W. Railway Branch to Holywell.

Scotchers Series.

The site of the mediaeval St Winefride's Well, the town of Trefynnon/Holywell has long been of some significance in north-east Wales. A place of pilgrimage in its own right, it is also the start of the pilgrimage route across north Wales to Ynys Enlli/Bardsea Island, 'the island of ten thousand saints'. However, in the nineteenth century it was not pilgrimages but a more prosaic consideration which brought about the creation of a railway. Limestone from Halkyn mountain was used locally for metal smelting and chemical production and textile mills had also sprung up around the town. The Holywell Railway, two miles in length, was authorised by an Act of July 1864 from Holywell to the London & North Western station on the Chester to Holyhead line. The undertaking was short-lived and was out of use by 1870. There was some interest in the route being taken over by a proposed branch of the Mersey Railway in 1873, but nothing came of this.

The opening of Holywell Station, 1 July 1912.

L & N.W. Railway Branch to Holywell. 7.

Scotcher's Series.

The line lay derelict until it was acquired by the LNWR in 1891, but they did nothing to develop it until a proposal was made to make it into an electric tramway; however, this did not materialise. It was not until 1 July 1912 that the line, rebuilt and realigned in places, was opened to goods and passengers. The branch was laid on a formidable gradient of 1 in 27 and was worked initially by auto trains comprising a tank engine and two converted picnic saloons. Working instructions for passengers and goods required the engine to be on the lower end of the train at all times, so goods trains were propelled up to the branch from the main line.

The line was provided with a generous passenger service, with up to 29 return journeys on Saturdays in the 1930s, but it was badly hit by bus competition and all services ceased from 6 September 1954. Goods traffic was worked to Crescent Siding, at the lower end of the line, until August 1957.

Prestatyn – Dyserth

Passenger service withdrawn	22 September 1930	*Station closed*	*Date of closure*
Distance	4½ miles	Meliden	22 September 1930
Original owning company	London & North Western Railway	Allt-y-Graig **	22 September 1930
		Dyserth	22 September 1930

Station closed	*Date of closure*
Chapel Street	22 September 1930
Woodland Park *	22 September 1930
St Melyd Golf Links	22 September 1930

*   Rhuddlan Road until 9 July 1923.
**   Originally named Alt-y-Craig until 8 July 1929.

Rhuddlan Road Halt.

LNWR steam rail motor at Rhuddlan Road Halt.

36473 PRESTATYN TO DYSERTH BY MOTOR

This short branch off the Chester to Holyhead route was originally promoted as a goods-only line in 1864, but nothing came of the scheme. Two years later, on 16 July 1866, the London & North Western Railway Act authorised the construction of a line for passengers and goods which would serve lead and haematite mines near Dyserth. The branch was single track with a passenger station at Rhyddlan Road. The line was opened in two stages, to Talargoch, where it served lead mines, in December 1867, and to Dyserth in March of the following year. In addition to Rhyddlan Road there was a goods station at Meliden.

A rail motor at Meliden. Note the warning sign in both English and Welsh to the right of the locomotive.

Rail Motor Car at MELIDEN.

Initially the passenger service was worked by an engine and carriages in the conventional manner, but from 28 August 1905 the LNWR introduced its new steam railmotors onto the branch. To increase traffic potential two new stations were provided, at Chapel Street, half a mile from Prestatyn, and at Meliden. Rhuddlan Road was renamed Woodland Park in 1923 when a new housing estate was built alongside the line. Further halts were added at St Melyn Golf Links in 1923 and Allt y Graig in 1928, but the passenger service was in stiff competition with the developing road transport and the London Midland Scottish withdrew it from 22 September 1930 as an economy when the Depression descended.

The crew of the rail motor pose beside it, just short of the station at Dyserth, which is out of shot on the right.

Goods services remained in operation into the post-war era, though Meliden closed completely in 1957. The line closed to regular traffic from 4 May 1964, but quarry traffic continued to Dyserth until 8 September 1973, the line being worked as a private siding. After this there was an attempt to re-open at least part of the line as a preservation project, though nothing came of this.

Rhiwabon/Ruabon – Legacy and Wrecsam/Wrexham – Wynn Hall

Passenger service withdrawn 22 March 1915 and 1 January 1931 (see text)
Distance Ruabon–Legacy: 3 miles
Wrexham–Wynn Hall: 5½ miles
Original owning company Great Western Railway /
North Wales Mineral Railway

Station closed	Date of closure
Ponkey Crossing Halt	22 March 1915
Aberderfyn Halt	22 March 1915

Station closed	Date of closure
Fennant Road Halt	22 March 1915
Rhostyllen	1 January 1931
Legacy	1 January 1931
Rhos (first station)	February 1855
Rhos (second station)	1 January 1931
Brook Street Halt	22 March 1915
Pant Halt	22 March 1915
Wynn Hall Halt	22 March 1915

Rhostyllen Station.

The area around Ruabon was extensively industrialised, not least due to the efforts of the Wynn family who had been prominent landowners in the area for generations and who were closely involved with the Great Western Railway. The London & North Western, through its ownership of the Shropshire Union Canal, also had a presence, though this was very much an island in a Great Western sea. A network of tramways connected to the canal and subsequently a number of goods-only railways were constructed, which formed a complex system serving collieries, ironworks, brickworks and chemical works.

Legacy Station, February 1949.

One of these goods lines was constructed by the Great Western in 1861 from Gardden Lodge Junction, north of Ruabon on the main line to Ponciau/Ponkey and Aberderfyn, a distance of 1¾ miles, later extended a further 1¼ miles to Legacy in 1871. Having been worked as a goods and mineral line for 25 years, in 1896 it was converted to carry passengers in order to counter a proposed East Denbighshire Railway, a project planned by the Wrexham, Mold & Connah's Quay Railway, then still independent, to create a line connecting Wrexham with Rhosllanerchrugog. The Great Western also constructed a connection at Legacy with the previously goods-only line to Pontcysyllte on the SUC, which was extended northwards to a new junction just south of Wrexham. The two lines were initially worked conventionally with engines and coaches but, like the lines to Berwig and Moss (see separate sections), steam railmotors were introduced from 1 May 1905, the Pontcysyllte line being reconstructed for passenger traffic as far south as a halt at Wynn Hall. As with other railmotor branches in the area, bus services eroded the trains' share of traffic and the Ruabon–Legacy section and the Pontcysyllte line south of Rhos were closed as a wartime economy in March 1915 and never reinstated. The Rhos line continued to carry passengers until the end of 1930 but then ceased to do so apart from occasional trains in connection with sporting events and eisteddfodau. Goods services continued to Pontcysyllte from Pant until 1953 and the line was further closed south of Rhos ten years later.

Rhiwabon/Ruabon – Dolgellau

Passenger service withdrawn	18 January 1965
Distance	45¼ miles
Original owning company	Vale of Llangollen Railway /
	Llangollen & Corwen Railway /
	Corwen & Bala Railway /
	Bala & Dolgelley Railway

Station closed	*Date of closure*
Acrefair	18 January 1965
Trevor	18 January 1965
Sun Bank Halt *	5 June 1950
Llangollen	18 January 1965
Berwyn Halt **	14 December 1964
Glyndyfrdwy	14 December 1964
Carrog	14 December 1964
Corwen ***	14 December 1964
Cynwyd	14 December 1964
Llandrillo	14 December 1964
Llandderfell ****	14 December 1964
Bala Junction	18 January 1965

Station closed	*Date of closure*
Bala Lake Halt †	25 September 1939
Llanuwchllyn ††	18 January 1965
Drws-y-Nant	18 January 1965
Bontnewydd	18 January 1965
Dolgellau †††	18 January 1965

*   Originally named Garth and Sun Bank Halt until 1 July 1906.
**   Originally named Berwyn until 20 September 1954.
***   Corwen had three stations in succession: the first, on the Denbigh, Ruthin & Corwen Railway, opened on 6 October 1864 and was replaced by a temporary station when the Llangollen & Corwen Railway opened on 1 May 1865. This was in turn replaced by a permanent station on 1 September 1865.
**** Originally named Llanderfel until 27 October 1908.
†   Reopened and renamed Bala (Llyn Tegid) on 25 March 1976.
††   Originally named Pandy until an unrecorded date. The station reopened on 14 August 1972.
†††   Originally named Dolgelly until 24 June 1896; then named Dolgelley until 12 September 1960.

Acrefair Station.

This section of cross-country railway was projected as a route to the west coast of Wales, branching off the Shrewsbury & Chester main line at Llangollen Line Junction, a little south of Ruabon. For much of its route it followed the old coaching road to Holyhead/Caergybi, latterly the A5, a route which gave abundant views of the scenery of mid Wales and the Snowdonia range. Unsurprisingly, given the significance of Holyhead as a packet port for Ireland, there were a number of unsuccessful schemes for railways which arose and vanished over the years before any rails were laid. Even so it is remarkable that four railway companies were involved in getting the line the 45¼ miles to Dolgellau and a further company, the Cambrian, was involved in actually building the line a further 7¾ miles to Barmouth Junction on the Coast line from Machynlleth to Pwllheli.

Llangollen Station, *c.* 1900.

The first part of the line was constructed by the Vale of Llangollen Railway, which received its Act of incorporation in August 1859. Thomas Brassey, the renowned contractor, was responsible for the four sections of line to Dolgellau and he began work on the Vale of Llangollen on 1 September 1859. The line was constructed as single track on a double formation and was opened to Llangollen for goods traffic from 1 December 1861 and for passengers on 2 June the following year.

Llangollen Station.

Beyond Llangollen construction was in the hands of the Llangollen & Corwen Railway, which received its Act in August 1860 and opened throughout on 8 May 1865. It made a junction with the Denbigh, Ruthin & Corwen Railway (see separate section) just east of the site of the permanent station at Corwen and from 11 October 1865 a second line of rails was laid alongside the original line to allow trains from Denbigh to run on their own route into the station.

Llangollen Station.

The third company, the Corwen & Bala, was the eventual outcome of a web of proposals for a line from Corwen to the coast in which the hand of Thomas Savin was much in evidence. Having promoted the Denbigh, Ruthin & Corwen line, he wished to link it to another of his companies, the Aberystwyth & Welch [*sic*] Coast Railway, near to Abermaw/Barmouth. There were also schemes to link Bala to the vale of Ffestiniog and Porthmadog and thereby tap the lucrative slate traffic of that area. Savin's schemes came to nothing, not least because the prospect of his influence over so large an area of northern Wales was simply unacceptable, not only to the railway companies but also to public opinion generally, and within a few years he disappeared from the railway scene after being declared bankrupt.

Glyndyfrdwy Station, *c.* 1905.

Glyndyfrdwy Station.

Both the Corwen & Bala and Bala & Dolgelley companies were authorised by Acts of June 1862. Trains began running between Corwen and Llandrillo from 16 July 1866, were extended to Bala on 1 April 1868 and Dolgellau on 4 August the same year. The remaining section, constructed by the Cambrian Railways, opened to Barmouth Junction on 11 June 1869, though the two companies had separate stations at Dolgelley until Cambrian trains began using the B&D station on 21 June.

The four independent companies entrusted the running of their lines to the Great Western from the outset. No doubt smarting from its inability to acquire the companies, which in 1865 amalgamated to form the Cambrian, it determined to have its own route to the west coast and moved quickly to secure it. The Cambrian was equally determined to prevent the Great Western from actually running onto its coast line and met it inland instead. In 1877 the GWR acquired the Bala & Dolgelley but it was 1896 before the other three companies entered its fold. In the fullness of time, at the Grouping, it also acquired the Cambrian Railways.

Corwen Station, *c.* **1910.**

The Ruabon–Dolgelley line was a popular route, serving not only the coast but also Llangollen, a celebrated inland destination for Victorian tourists. In 1882 the line from Bala across the mountains to Blaenau Ffestiniog was opened, the junction between it and the coast route creating Bala Junction, one of a number of such stations in Wales. Remote from any settlement - Bala was 55 chains further on - it had no road access and no goods yard but was simply an interchange point between the two lines; other examples included Afon Wen, Talyllyn, Three Cocks and Barmouth Junction. Through trains to the coast were run from Paddington in the summer and the line conveyed a heavy seasonal traffic in pre-motor days.

Corwen West Signal box surrounded by floodwater. The Dee Valley is prone to flooding, which occasionally inundated the railway and ultimately caused its closure. *The Barmouth & County Advertiser* reported an incident on 17 September 1903: 'On Tuesday night of last week one of the severest storms of recent years raged, and on Wednesday morning the whole Valley of the Dee from Bala to Corwen was one vast lake.'

The post-war years of the mid-twentieth century saw a gradual decline in traffic, seasonal travellers deserting the railway for motor coaches and cars. Goods services west of Llangollen ended in 1964 and in December of that year floods breached the line near Dolgellau and east of Bala. Passenger services finally ceased from 18 January 1965, though goods services between Ruabon and Llangollen soldiered on until 1 January 1968.

Cynwyd Station, *c.* 1905.

Yet this was not the end for the line. Two sections have been reopened by preservation groups, that between Llanuwchllyn and Bala Lake Halt along the shore of Llyn Tegid/Bala Lake as a 1' 11½" gauge line as Rheilffordd Llyn Tegid/Bala Lake Railway in August 1972, and the section from Llangollen westwards as the standard gauge Rheilffordd Llangollen/Llangollen Railway from 1975. Over the years it has progressed further, reaching Carrog in 1996 and Corwen in 2014. The coast may be a long way off, but the line still lives!

Llandrillo Station, c. 1905.

Bala Junction Station, 1933.

Rhyl – Dynbych/Denbigh – Corwen

Passenger service withdrawn	19 September 1955 (Rhyl–Denbigh)	*Station closed*	*Date of closure*
	2 February 1953 (Denbigh–Corwen)	Rhewl	30 April 1962
Distance	30 miles	Ruthin	30 April 1962
Original owning company	Vale of Clwyd Railway /	Eyarth	2 February 1953
	Denbigh, Ruthin & Corwen Railway	Nantclwyd	2 February 1953
		Derwen	2 February 1953
		Gwyddelwern	2 February 1953
Station closed		Corwen (first station) *	1 September 1865
Rhuddlan	*Date of closure*	Corwen (second station)	14 December 1964
St Asaph	19 September 1955		
Trefnant	19 September 1955		
Denbigh	19 September 1955		
Llanrhiadr	1 March 1962		
	2 February 1953		

*   Temporary station, replaced by the second one on the opening of the connection between GW and DR&C lines).

Rhuddlan Station.

St Asaph Station.

This line formed a north-south connection between the Chester & Holyhead main line and the Ruabon–Dolgellau line, both of which ran east-west. Originally promoted as two separate companies, the first, the Vale of Clwyd, was authorised by Act of Parliament in June 1856, after several previous schemes for lines in the same area had come to nothing. The engineer was Benjamin Piercy and the contractor David Davies of Llandinam, both having long associations with railways in mid Wales and the borders. The line was opened on 5 October 1858, access to Rhyl being at the goodwill of the London & North Western as successors to the Chester & Holyhead. The Vale of Clwyd line, single track throughout, diverged from the main line at Foryd where for some years there was a harbour owned by Hugh Robert Hughes of Kinmel Hall, who ran a steamer service to Liverpool.

TROOPS DETRAINING AT TREFNANT.

Y.M.C.A. No 20,

The southward extension of the line to meet the Ruabon–Dolgellau route at Corwen was undertaken by the Denbigh, Ruthin & Corwen Railway, authorised by Parliament in 1863. Although it never ultimately fulfilled these hopes, it was promoted as the first stage of a line towards Bala, which was eventually constructed later by the independent Corwen & Bala Railway (see separate section).

Denbigh Station, 1908.

The line opened as far as Gwyddelwern in 1862, but the section on to Corwen was delayed by the need to construct the 300-foot long viaduct across the Dyfrdwy/Dee valley outside of Corwen. There were also troubles caused largely by the intransigence of the contractor, Thomas Savin, David Davies' former partner, who had been paid for much of his work in shares and was in a commanding position with the board. However, by 1864 the London & North Western had taken over the operation of the two lines and Savin discovered that Euston could be as intransigent as he, if not more so. Trains initially ran into a temporary station at Corwen from 6 October 1864, the last quarter-mile into the GWR station being opened from 1 September in the following year.

The Vale of Clwyd line was absorbed by the LNWR from 15 July 1867 and the Denbigh, Ruthin & Corwen from 3 July 1879. The route never carried heavy traffic and with the opening of the Mold & Denbigh Junction Railway (see separate section) it was increasingly worked in two sections, Rhyl–Denbigh and Chester–Corwen.

Rhewl Station, May 1961, looking neglected though surprisingly intact after the line had been closed to passengers

The lines closed to passengers from 2 February 1953 and 19 September 1955 respectively. However, this was not the end of passenger traffic as the line was used for excursions making for the coast of Cardigan Bay and also for the popular 'North Wales Land Cruise' trains, which ran during the summer months up to 1962. The Ruthin–Corwen section closed completely from 30 April 1962, Denbigh–Ruthin suffering the same fate from 1 March 1965. Rhyl–Denbigh finally lost its goods services from 1 January 1968.

Ruthin Station, May 1961.

Whitchurch – Oswestry – Buttington *

Passenger service withdrawn	18 January 1965		
Distance	31¼ miles		
Original owning company	Oswestry, Ellesmere & Whitchurch Railway		
	(Whitchurch –Oswestry)		
	Oswestry & Newtown Railway (Oswestry – Buttington)		

* The closed stations on this line that were in Shropshire were Welshampton, Ellesmere, Frankton, Whittington, Oswestry, Llynclys, Pant and Llanymynech. The closed stations that were in Montgomeryshire were Four Crosses, Arddleen, Pool Quay, and Buttington Junction.

Station closed	*Date of closure*
Fenns Bank	18 January 1965
Bettisfield	18 January 1965

By the early 1850s most of the main elements of the British railway network either existed or were in process of construction, but certain areas of the country were significantly less well covered than others. These included a good deal of Scotland north of the central belt and most of mid-Wales, where railway communication was every bit as important as elsewhere, though finance was hard to raise. The large English companies, like the London & North Western and the Great Western, showed little significant interest in mid-Wales – though this was to change during the following decade – and so it was left to local initiative to promote a railway across the centre of Wales, following the valley of the Severn for much of its distance, with the aim of linking Aberystwyth to the LNWR line from Shrewsbury to Crewe at Whitchurch.

The story of the development of what became in 1865 the Cambrian Railways – the plural is significant – has often been told; but the section which concerns this book is that between Whitchurch and Buttington, just north-east of Welshpool. This was constructed by the Oswestry & Newtown Railway, which had been authorised by Parliament on 26 June 1855 and opened in two sections in May and August 1860 between Newtown and Welshpool; and by the Oswestry, Ellesmere and Whitchurch Railway, authorised on 1 August 1861 and opened, again in two sections, in May 1863 and July 1864. This allowed the developing network through mid-Wales to be linked to the rest of the national network at two points, Whitchurch and, after 1862, Shrewsbury, the latter through the notionally independent Shrewsbury & Welshpool Railway. This was backed and initially worked by the London & North Western and Great Western companies and was later taken over by them both as a joint line, connection with the Oswestry & Newtown being made at Buttington.

For a century these arrangements continued, much of the traffic onto the Cambrian system originating initially on the LNWR, though after the Grouping of 1923 the Cambrian became a constituent company of the reconstituted Great Western. This probably tipped the balance of traffic in the latter's favour and by the time the Beeching Report emerged in 1963, the section between Buttington and Whitchurch was proposed for closure, the Cambrian system's sole connection with the rest of British Railways henceforth being from Shrewsbury. A certain amount of pruning had already happened, as the closure dates of the stations along the route through Oswestry indicate. Oswestry, formerly the Cambrian headquarters and works, lost its passenger service completely with the cessation of the service over the former Great Western route from Gobowen. However, the line was left between Gobowen and Porthywaun, on the former Tanat Valley Light Railway, to serve limestone quarries which supplied the railway with ballast. The track is still there, though badly overgrown. Preservation has sprung up too, both in Oswestry itself and further south, at Llynclys. This lost section of the Cambrian still sees trains occasionally, some steam hauled.

Wrecsam/Wrexham – Berwig

Passenger service withdrawn	27 March 1950 (see text)
Distance	6¾ miles
Original owning company	Wrexham & Minera Railway

Station closed	*Date of closure*
Plas Power	1 January 1931
The Lodge Halt	1 January 1931
Brymbo	27 March 1950

Station closed	*Date of closure*
Brymbo West Crossing Halt	1 January 1931
Pentresaeson for Bwlchgwyn Halt	1 January 1931
Coed Poeth	1 January 1931
Vicarage Crossing Halt *	1 January 1931
Berwig Halt *	1 January 1931

*   Closed temporarily from 1 January to 2 April 1917.

Plas Power Station, *c.* **1903.**

Minera, a little over three miles due west of Wrexham, was an important source of limestone and from July 1847 was connected to the Shrewsbury & Chester line at Wheatsheaf Junction by a 6¼-mile line of the North Wales Mineral Railway, which included an inclined plane. The NWMR served a number of collieries in the Minera area as well as other extractive industries. The Wrexham & Minera Railway's line from Croes Newydd, constructed in 1865 (see separate section), linked up with the NWMR line and allowed the Great Western access to Minera.

Brymbo Station, *c.* 1908.

Until 15 November 1897 the Wrexham & Minera line beyond Brymbo towards Minera was goods only, but on that day passenger services began as far as Coed Poeth and from May 1905 the passenger service was extended to Berwig. Conventional trains of engines and coaches were used initially but from March 1905 steam railmotors were introduced and halts were provided at Brymbo West Crossing, Pentresaeson, Vicarage Crossing and Berwig. The railmotors must have found the going difficult on the gradients and passenger receipts must have been modest on the far section of the line as services were temporarily suspended beyond Coed Poeth in the early months of 1917. Passenger services fell victim to bus competition after the Great War and were fatally undermined by the Depression after 1929, being withdrawn from the first day of 1931. However, the line survived for over four decades after this, reverting to goods traffic only.

BERWIG STATION

Wrecsam/Wrexham – Brymbo

Passenger service withdrawn	1 March 1917	*Station closed*		*Date of closure*
Distance	4¼ miles *	Moss and Pentre		1 March 1917
Original owning company	Wrexham, Mold & Connah's Quay Railway	New Broughton Road Halt		1 March 1917
		Plas Power		1 March 1917
Station closed	*Date of closure*	Brymbo		1 March 1917
Rhosddu Halt	1 March 1917			
Highfield Road Halt	1 March 1917	* Distance from Wrexham Exchange; 4¾ miles from Wrexham Central.		

The Wrexham, Mold & Connah's Quay Railway was very much a feature of the railway history of the industrial area of north-east Wales and went through a complex series of projected and actual developments, setbacks and reversals of fortune. It always operated on a shoestring budget; in his seminal history of the Great Central Railway, which absorbed the WM&CQ in 1905, George Dow described the line as 'a ramshackle railway'. The GCR set about reorganising, modernising and extending its main line to link up with lines in the Wirral and the Cheshire Lines Committee.

As a major ironmaking centre surrounded by the coalfield, Brymbo had already attracted the London & North Western and Great Western companies (see separate sections) when in 1882 the WM&CQ was authorised to construct a short single-track branch from a junction at Rhosddu, north of its Wrexham Exchange station, to the town with stations at Moss & Pentre and Plas Power, where there was a junction with the Wrexham & Minera route. The line was opposed determinedly by the Great Western, but was opened on 1 August 1889. After the Great Central acquired the WM&CQ in 1905 two halts were opened at Rhosddu and Highfield Road and a further one at New Broughton Road in the following year. The GC also worked the line with steam railmotors from their introduction in 1905, taking a leaf out of the Great Western's book, but they met with no more success and the service was withdrawn on 1 March 1917. The line to Brymbo remained in use for goods up to the 1970s, but the passenger station gradually disappeared, overwhelmed by the waste tips from the steelworks.

Wrecsam/Wrexham – Moss

Passenger service withdrawn	1 January 1931
Distance	3¼ miles
Original owning company	Great Western Railway
Station closed	*Date of closure*
Gatewen Halt	1 January 1931
Pentre Broughton Halt	1 January 1931
Gwersyllt Hill Halt	1 January 1931
Moss Platform	1 January 1931

This short branch left the Wrexham & Minera line around three-quarters of a mile beyond the junction at Croes Newydd and struck off northwards to an end-on connection with the Wrexham, Mold & Connah's Quay line in the area of Ffrwd ironworks. There has been some debate about the date of opening, some sources giving May 1881 and others March 1882. It remained a goods-only route until 1 May 1905 when the Great Western began a passenger service which, like the Berwig branch, was operated by steam railmotors. Halts were provided at Gatewen, Pentre Broughton and Gwersyllt Hill (presumably so named to distinguish it from Gwersyllt on the WM&CQ line, now owned by the Great Central) and passenger services ended at Moss Platform, an unusual though not unique example of a terminus which was also a halt. As with the Berwig line, road competition after 1918 proved its undoing and passenger trains ceased on the same day in 1931.

Yr Wyddgrug/Mold – Brymbo

Passenger service withdrawn	27 March 1950	*Station closed*	*Date of closure*
Distance	8½ miles	Coed Talon	27 March 1950
Original owning company	London & North Western Railway /	Llanfynydd	27 March 1950
	Great Western Railway /	Ffrith	27 March 1950
	Wrexham & Minera Joint Railway	Brymbo	27 March 1950

Coed Talon Station.

Coed Talon Station

The construction of the Mold Railway had brought steam powered passenger lines - and the London & North Western Railway - into the industrial area around the Dee estuary. A branch, mainly for the carriage of minerals, had been opened at the same time as the Mold Railway's main line in 1849 to serve collieries in the Coed Talon area and in 1851 a station at Padeswood had been opened at the point where the branch diverged.

Llanfynydd Halt.

It was most improbable that the LNWR would not use its presence to promote lines southwards towards Wrexham, though initially it was the independent Mold & Denbigh Junction Railway which tried to construct a line. However, in May 1861 the Wrexham & Minera Railway was incorporated to build a 3¼-mile goods line from Croes Newydd on the Shrewsbury & Chester line just south of Wrexham to Brymbo, where there were considerable ironworks. It opened in May 1862. There then followed a protracted battle between a number of schemes aiming to promote railways into the coalfield, with the LNWR intent on reaching Wrexham and the Great Western equally intent on reaching Mold and neither company being willing to yield to the other. Into this 'war of all against all' came George Hammond Whalley, the brothers Benjamin and Robert Piercy, and Thomas Savin, the latter still solvent, all long-term protagonists in railway schemes in the area. A further railway interest was the newly-constructed Wrexham, Mold & Connah's Quay Railway, a line which was to feature prominently in the district and, despite being beset by many difficulties, has long outlasted others in this book.

When the dust settled on these proposals and counter-proposals, the Wrexham & Minera managed to obtain powers in July 1865 to extend its line from Brymbo to an end-on connection with the LNWR Ffrith branch at Coed Talon. An attempt to open it for passenger traffic in July 1866 failed when the Board of Trade inspector declined to pass it as serviceable and in the previous month the Brymbo–Coed Talon line was vested jointly in the LNWR and the Great Western, becoming the Wrexham & Minera Joint. It opened to goods in January 1872. From 1 January a passenger service commenced between Mold and Brymbo and in 1910 this consisted of four return journeys a day with an additional return journey on Wednesdays and Saturdays and no Sunday service. Passengers for Wrexham changed at Brymbo, so the Great Western was spared having to accommodate LNWR passenger trains at Wrexham. The service continued until March 1950, though goods and particularly mineral traffic remained in the Brymbo area well into the 1970s.

Stations closed on lines still open to passengers:
Chester – Bangor

Original owning company	Chester & Holyhead Railway

Stations closed	Date of closure
Sandycroft	1 May 1961
Queensferry *	14 February 1966
Connah's Quay	14 February 1966
Bagillt (first station) **	1871
Bagillt (second station)	14 February 1966
Holywell Junction ***	14 February 1966
Mostyn	14 February 1966
Talacre	14 February 1966
Foryd (first station)	20 April 1885
Kinmel Bay Halt ****	2 September 1939
Llandulas (second station)	1 December 1952
Llysfaen †	5 January 1931

Station closed	Date of closure
Old Colwyn ††	1 December 1952
Mochdre & Pabo †††	5 January 1931
Aber	12 September 1960

*   Originally named Queen's Ferry (date of name change not recorded).
**   Originally named Bagilt until *c.* 1860.
***   Originally named Holywell until 1 July 1912.
**** Originally named Foryd (second station) until closure on 5 January 1931 (temporarily closed between 2 July 1917 and 1 July 1919). Reopened as Kinmel Bay Halt on 4 June 1938.
†   Originally named Llandulas (first station) until 1 July 1889.
††   Originally named Colwyn until 1 June 1885.
†††   Closed temporarily between 1 January 1917 and 5 May 1919.

Connah's Quay Station, 1904.

Shrewsbury – Chester *

Original owning company
Shrewsbury & Chester Railway

Stations closed
Cefn
Johnstown & Hafod
Rhosrobin Halt
Gresford for Llay Halt **
Rossett

Date of closure
12 September 1960
12 September 1960
6 October 1947
10 September 1962
29 October 1964

Station closed
Balderton

Date of closure
3 March 1953

* Closed stations on this line that were in Shropshire were Leaton, Baschurch, Rednal and West Felton, Whittington Low level and Weston Rhyn. The closed station on the line that was in Cheshire was Saltney.

** Originally named Gresford until 1932 and then Gresford for Llay until 2 May 1955.

Johnstown & Hafod Halt, May 1961. In the background are the spoil heaps of Hafod-y-Bwch Colliery.

Wrecsam/Wrexham – Shotton

Original owning company   Wrexham, Mold & Connah's Quay Railway

Stations closed   *Date of closure*
Hope High Level *   1 September 1958

*   Originally named Hope Exchange (Great Central Railway) until 7 November 1953.

Hope High Level Station, May 1955.